# DINOSAUR
## CODE CRACKERS

**Highlights Press**
**Honesdale, Pennsylvania**

# DINO-MITE JOKES

The punch lines to these jokes are written in code. Using the decoder wheel, find the letter that matches the number under each blank space. Fill in the blanks until all the hidden punch lines are revealed.

For this puzzle, line up **S** with **26** on the decoder wheel.

What did the green dinosaur say to the purple dinosaur?

D r e a _ _ _ _
9  25  12  8  1  15  12

What kind of music do paleontologists like?

_ _ _ _
25  22  10  18

What do you ask a thirsty tyrannosaur?

_ _ _ , _ _ _ ?
1  12  8   25  12  5

What side of a dinosaur has the most scales?

_ _ _   _ _ _ _ _ _ _
1  15  12   22  2  1  26  16  11  12

**FUN FACT:** *T. rex* teeth were the size of bananas.

hese dinosaur
ddles are real
ead-scratchers.
And so are the
nswers to the
ddles—that's
because they're
written in code! Read
ach riddle and try to
uess its answer. Then
se the decoder wheel
o reveal if your guesses
were right.

# RIP-ROARING RIDDLES

For this puzzle, line up
**K** with **22**
on the decoder wheel.

## RIDDLE 1

I walk on all fours and
eat plants to survive.
I have lots of plates but
no forks or knives.

### WHO AM I?

## RIDDLE 2

Don't make us scrambled,
boiled, or fried—not when
there are dinosaurs inside!

### WHAT ARE WE?

4   5   16   18   26   4   12   6   3   6   4        16   18   18   4

## RIDDLE 3

When it comes to food,
it's clear what I eat. At
mealtimes, I like to chow
down on meat.

### WHAT AM I?

14   12   3   25   20   7   26   3   16

# HIDDEN PICTURES

There are eight objects hidden in the big picture. And each object name is hidden behind a code! Use the decoder wheel to uncov[er] each object name. Once you've decoded them all, find the objects in the picture.

**For this puzzle, line up T with 6 on the decoder wheel.**

15 13 4 4 1 6

24 1 24 24 21 2 1 2

2 21 12 12 13

9 20 17 17 24

18 21 5 20

14 1 1 6

25 7 19

18 24 1 9 17 4

**TONGUE TWISTER:** *T. rex* tried trick-or-treating.

**FUN FACT:** Dinosaur fossils have been found on every continent, including Antarctica.

## ⊰BONUS⊱

Read down the highlighted letters from the list
of objects to get the answer to the riddle below:

**Why is *Therizinosaurus* always showing off its long claws?**

**Because they're** ___ ___ ___ ___ - ___ ___ ___ ___!

# WORD FOR WORDS

The letters in **TRICERATOPS** can make many other words. Clues to some of these words are below. But parts of the clues are in code! Use the decoder wheel to figure out the missing pieces of each clue. Then figure out the words based on the hints. We've done the first one for you.

For this puzzle, line up **W** with **18** on the decoder wheel.

## TRICERATOPS

**1.** A large R O D E N T       R A T
13 10 25 26 9 15

**2.** It __ __ __ __ __ to communicate.
8 26 10 18 14

**3.** This keeps drinks __ __ __ __
24 10 7 25

**4.** A __ __ __ __ __ that's often green.
1 13 16 4 15

**5.** You __ __ __ __ with them.
3 26 22 13

**6.** Superheroes __ __ __ __ them.
18 26 22 13

## ⪢ BONUS ⪡
How many other words can you make from **TRICERATOPS**? Set a timer for two minutes. Then write down as many additional words as you can. When the time is up, compare your word list to the lists of other players. Whoever comes up with the most words wins!

These dinosaur-related words are written in code—and jumbled! Use the decoder wheel to decipher each set of letters. Then unscramble the letters to find all six words.

# DINOSAUR SCRAMBLES

For this puzzle, line up
**C** with **1**
on the decoder wheel.

| Read the Wheel | Decode the Letters | Unscramble the Words |
|---|---|---|
| 21  8  25  17 | | |
| 16 18 3 7 10 3 14 | | |
| 18 22 7 1 12 3 18 | | |
| 26 12 3 13 17 | | |
| 7 5 2 | | |
| 8 16 7 25 17 17 19 1 | | |

# DINO-MITE JOKES

The punch lines to these jokes are written in code. Using the decoder wheel, find the letter that matches the number under each blank space. Fill in the blanks until all the hidden punch lines are revealed.

For this puzzle, line up L with 15 on the decoder wheel.

What did the dinosaur use to make hot dogs?

___ ___ ___ ___ ___ ___ ___ ___   ___ ___ ___ ___
13  24  21  4   22  22  12  6     19  18  21  14

What dinosaur loves astrology?

___ ___ ___ ___-___ ___ ___ ___ ___ ___ ___
22  14  2   6   8   21  4   23  18  19  22

What did *Stegosaurus* say after making a mess in the kitchen?

" ___ ___ ___ ___-___ ___ ___ ___ ___!"
  7   12  17  18  22  18  21  21  2

What do you call a dinosaur who snores?

___ ___ ___ ___ ___ ___-___-___ ___ ___ ___ ___ ___
4   22  17  18  21  8   4   22  4   24  21  24  22

**FUN FACT:** *Pachycephalosaurus* skulls were 20 times thicker than those of other dinosaurs.

Owen the *Oviraptor* wrote a letter to his pal Drake the *Diplodocus* about a concert he saw. But parts of the letter are written in code. Use the decoder wheel to complete the letter. Then read the letter aloud.

# DEAR DINOSAUR

For this puzzle, line up **R** with **4** on the decoder wheel.

Dear Drake the *Diplodocus*,

I saw a ___ ___ ___ ___ - ___ ___ ___ ___ concert today. First, a group of
     4   1   13   4      5   1   25   17

___ ___ ___ ___ ___ ___ ___ took the stage. Then a ___ ___ ___ ___ -
4  13  2  6  1  4  5            16  21  26  1

___ ___ ___ ___ ___ ___ sang. Finally, there was ___ ___ ___ ___ music.
15  20  1  4  7  5            22  13  9  5

Everyone was super ___ ___ ___ ___ ___ - ___ ___ ___. Next time, you'll have
           6  13  24  1  26   6  17  16

___ ___ ___ ___ ___ come along.
6  1  1  6  20

Yours ptero-ly,
Owen the *Oviraptor*

# HIDDEN PICTURES

There are eight objects hidden in the big picture. And each object name is hidden behind a code! Use the decoder wheel to uncov each object name. Once you've decoded them all, finc the objects in the picture.

For this puzzle, line up
**Y** with **18**
on the decoder wheel.

___ ___ ___ ___ ___ ___ ___ ___
12  20  14  22  24   9  20   7

___ ___ ___ ___ ___ ___
6   20   5   5  24  13

___ ___ ___ ___ ___
22  11   8  16   7

___ ___ ___ ___ ___ ___ ___ ___ ___ ___
21   2   7   8  22  14   5  20  11  12

___ ___ ___ ___
22   8   6  21

___ ___ ___ ___ ___ ___ ___ ___ ___ ___ ___ ___
22  11  24  12  22  24   7  13   6   8   8   7

___ ___ ___ ___ ___
11  14   5  24  11

___ ___ ___ ___
12   1   8  24

**TONGUE TWISTER:**
Dazzling dinosaurs dance delightedly.

**FUN FACT:** Some dinosaur species were covered in feathers.

## ⋛BONUS⋚

Read down the highlighted letters from the list
of objects to get the answer to the riddle below:

**Why do museums have old dinosaur bones?**

**They can't afford** ___ ___ ___   ___ ___ ___ ___ ___ !

# WORD FOR WORDS

For this puzzle, line up **G** with **16** on the decoder wheel.

The letters in **MEGALOSAURUS** can make many other words. Clues to some of these words are below. But parts of the clues are in code! Use the decoder wheel to figure out the missing pieces of each clue. Then figure out the words based on the hints.

# MEGALOSAURUS

**1.** Something you ___ ___ ___ ___
12 17 14 6

___ ___ ___

**2.** Your ___ ___ ___ ___ ___ limbs
21 24 6 14 1

___ ___ ___

**3.** A ___ ___ ___ ___ ___ ___ art supply
2 3 18 12 20 8

___ ___ ___

**4.** ___ ___ ___ , chess, or hide-and-seek
3 10 16

___ ___ ___

**5.** A big painting on a ___ ___ ___ ___
6 10 21 21

___ ___ ___

**6.** You ___ ___ ___ three a day.
14 10 3

___ ___ ___

## ≷BONUS≷

How many other words can you make from **MEGALOSAURUS**? Set a timer for two minutes. Then write down as many additional words as you can. When the time is up, compare your word list to the lists of other players. Whoever comes up with the most words wins!

**12 FUN FACT:** A dinosaur known as *Yi qi* only grew to be the size of a pigeon!

How do you tell a dinosaur that you think it's swell? Use the decoder wheel to reveal these raw-some dinosaur compliments.

# DINOSAUR COMPLIMENTS

For this puzzle, line up
X with 7
on the decoder wheel.

8 24 4'1 14   3.   1 14 7 - 14 21 21 14 23 3!

_____

18'22   14 23 – 1 10 25 3 24 1 – 14 13   11 8   8 24 4.

_____

18   13 18 16   8 24 4.

_____

8 24 4   22 10 20 14   22 8   17 14 10 1 3   2 10 4 1.

_____

23 24 3 17 18 23 16   3 1 18 12 14 1 10 3 24 25 2   8 24 4!

# ⋛BONUS⋚

Line up the letter A with any number you choose on the decoder wheel. Use this code to write a compliment to a friend or family member. Have them use the decoder wheel to decipher your note.

# DINO-MITE JOKES

The punch lines to these jokes are written in code. Using the decoder wheel, find the letter that matches the number under each blank space. Fill in the blanks until all the hidden punch lines are revealed.

For this puzzle, line up **A** with **23** on the decoder wheel.

How do baby dinosaurs hatch?

\_\_ \_\_ \_\_ \_\_ \_\_ \_\_ \_\_ \_\_ - \_\_ \_\_.
16   4   1   21    1   3   3   15    5   16

What did the *T. rex* wish for when he blew out his candles?

\_\_ \_\_ \_\_ \_\_ \_\_ \_\_ \_\_ \_\_ \_\_ \_\_
8   11   10   3   1   14   23   14   9   15

What did the fossil bring to dinner?

\_\_ \_\_ \_\_ \_\_ \_\_ \_\_ \_\_ \_\_ \_\_
15   12   23   14   1    14   5   24   15

What is a paleontologist's favorite book?

\_\_ \_\_ \_\_ \_\_ \_\_ \_\_ - \_\_ \_\_ \_\_ \_\_ \_\_ \_\_ \_\_
16   4   1   26   5   3    16   5   11   10   23   14   21

**FUN FACT:** *T. rex* jaws could have crushed a car with one bite.

These dinosaur riddles are real head-scratchers. And so are the answers to the riddles—that's because they're written in code! Read each riddle and try to guess its answer. Then use the decoder wheel to reveal if your guesses were right.

# RIP-ROARING RIDDLES

For this puzzle, line up
U with 11
on the decoder wheel.

## RIDDLE 1

Scientists dig me.
They think that I rock.
They study me, looking for
secrets to unlock.

### WHAT AM I?

— — — — — —
22  5  9  9  25  2

## RIDDLE 2

I hang out in rivers for much
of the time, with my long,
fish-like tail and a back
lined with spines.

### WHO AM I?

— — — — — — — — — — —
9  6  25  4  5  9  17  11  8  11  9

## RIDDLE 3

I love my name.
It has a nice ring.
All who hear it know
that I'm king.

### WHO AM I?

— — — — — — — — — — — — — —
0  15  8  17  4  4  5  9  17  11  8  11  9  8  21  14

**FUN FACT:** Ankylosaurus was covered with hard plates. Even on its eyelids!

15

# HIDDEN PICTURES

There are seven objects hidden in the big picture. And each object name is hidden behind a code! Use the decoder wheel to uncover each object name. Once you decoded them all, find the objects in the picture.

For this puzzle, line up **D** with **10** on the decoder wheel.

**TONGUE TWISTER:** Brave *Brontosaurus* babies break branches.

___ ___ ___ ___ ___ ___ ___
12  11  7   26  14  11  24

___ ___ ___ ___ ___ ___ ___ ___
25  9   15  25  25  21  24  25

___ ___ ___ ___ ___ ___ ___ ___ ___
14  21  24  25  11  25  14  21  11

___ ___ ___ ___ ___ ___ ___
22  11  20  20  7   20  26

___ ___ ___ ___ ___
13  18  21  2   11

___ ___ ___ ___
24  15  20  13

___ ___ ___ ___ ___  ___ ___ ___ ___
22  7   24  26  5    14  7   26

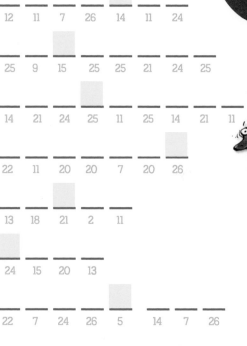

**FUN FACT:** *Diplodocus* brains were only slightly bigger than a walnut.

## ≡BONUS≡

Read down the highlighted letters from the list
of objects to get the answer to the riddle below:

**Why was school easier for the dinosaurs?**

Because there was not much __ __ __ __ __ __ __ to study.

# WORD FOR WORDS

The letters in **BRACHIOSAURUS** can make many other words. Clues to some of these words are below. But parts of the clues are in code! Use the decoder wheel to figure out the missing pieces of each clue. Then figure out the words based on the hints.

For this puzzle, line up **I** with **12** on the decoder wheel.

# BRACHIOSAURUS

**1.** A baby ___ ___ ___ ___
 5  8  4  21
        ___ ___ ___ ___

**2.** A ___ ___ ___ ___ ___ ___ ride to school
 2  8  15  15  18  26
        ___ ___ ___ ___

**3.** The person in ___ ___ ___ ___ ___ ___
 6  11  4  21  10  8
        ___ ___ ___ ___

**4.** ___ ___ ___ ___ ___ minutes
 22  12  1  23  2
        ___ ___ ___ ___

**5.** What a ___ ___ ___ ___ sleeps in
 5  4  5  2
        ___ ___ ___ ___

**6.** A type of ___ ___ ___ ___ ___
 22  17  4  14  8
        ___ ___ ___ ___

## ≥BONUS≤

How many other words can you make from **BRACHIOSAURUS**? Set a timer for two minutes. Then write down as many additional words as you can. When the time is up, compare your word list to the lists of other players. Whoever comes up with the most words wins!

**FUN FACT:** In 2010, scientists discovered the fossil of a 15-horned dinosaur in Utah.

These dinosaur-related words are written in code—and jumbled! Use the decoder wheel to decipher each set of letters. Then unscramble the letters to find all six words.

# DINOSAUR SCRAMBLES

For this puzzle, line up **M** with **18** on the decoder wheel.

| Read the Wheel | Decode the Letters | Unscramble the Words |
|---|---|---|
| 24 8 17 10 6 24 | | |
| 8 2 17 24 6 | | |
| 24 14 11 17 24 20 | | |
| 13 23 19 20 | | |
| 25 24 6 14 24 14 23 8 | | |
| 12 10 12 24 | | |

# DINO-MITE JOKES

The punch lines to these jokes are written in code. Using the decoder wheel, find the letter that matches the number under each blank space. Fill in the blanks until all the hidden punch lines are revealed.

**For this puzzle, line up L with 24 on the decoder wheel.**

What do you call a dinosaur who hates losing?

___ ___ ___ ___ ___ ___ ___ ___ ___ ___
13   5   13  7   4   24  1   5   17  4

What do you call a dinosaur who knows a lot of words?

___ ___ ___ ___ ___ ___ ___ ___ ___ ___
13   6   20  17  5   13  7   4   7   5

What's a dinosaur's least favorite reindeer?

___ ___ ___ ___ ___
15   1   25  17  6

What do you call a dinosaur who just ran a marathon?

___ ___ ___ ___ - ___ ___ ___ ___
16   21  26  1      5   1   4   17

**FUN FACT:** Scientists found ancient footprints from a baby *Apatosaurus* in Colorado in 2010

Eddie the *Edmontosaurus* wrote a thank-you note to his grandmother. But parts of the letter are written in code. Use the decoder wheel to complete the letter. Then read the letter aloud.

# DEAR DINOSAUR

For this puzzle, line up **F** with **23** on the decoder wheel.

Dear Grandma,

Thank you for my ___ ___ ___ ___ ___ -day gift! I was so
25  18  11  20  25

___ ___ ___ - ___ ___ ___ ___ ___ to get tickets to the Dinosaur Sports
22  24  24     20  26  11  22  21

___ ___ ___ ___ ___ - ___ ___ ___ ___ ___ ___ ___ ! I had so much
20  25  6  4  7     26  6  5  10  25  26  7

fun, and my team ___ ___ ___ ___ -ed to victory. I ___ ___ ___ ___
                  10  18  12  9                    4  26  10  10

you and hope you ___ ___ ___ ___ ___ by for a visit soon!
                 10  11  6  4  7

Love,
Eddie the *Edmontosaurus*

# HIDDEN PICTURES

There are eight objects hidden in the big picture. And each object name is hidden behind a code! Use the decoder wheel to uncover each object name. Once you've decoded them all, find the objects in the picture.

For this puzzle, line up
**C with 7**
on the decoder wheel.

___ ___ ___
6   5   24

___ ___ ___ ___ ___ ___ ___ ___
23  5  13  16   6  19   5  24

___ ___ ___ ___ ___
12  9   5  22  24

___ ___ ___ ___ ___ ___
6  19  24  24  16   9

___ ___ ___ ___ ___ ___
17 13  24  24   9  18

___ ___ ___ ___ ___ ___
7   5  18   8  16   9

___ ___ ___ ___ ___ ___ ___ ___ ___
16 13  11  12  24   6  25  16   6

___ ___ ___ ___ ___
11 16  19  26   9

**TONGUE TWISTER:**
Stanley, I'm certain that *Stegosaurus* saw us.

**FUN FACT:** The neck of *Mamenchisaurus* was nearly the length of a school bus.

≳BONUS≲

Read down the highlighted letters from the list
of objects to get the answer to the riddle below:

**Why did carnivorous dinosaurs eat their meat raw?**

:cause they didn't know how to _ _ _ _ _ _ _

# WORD FOR WORDS

The letters in **IGUANODON** can make many other words. Clues to some of these words are below. But parts of the clues are in code! Use the decoder wheel to figure out the missing pieces of each clue. Then figure out the words based on the hints.

For this puzzle, line up **Y** with **14** on the decoder wheel.

## IGUANODON

1. A ___ ___ ___ -person group
   9   12   4
   ___ ___ ___

2. It ___ ___ ___ ___ ___ .
   12   4   4   21   8
   ___ ___ ___ ___

3. Use a ___ ___ ___ ___ ___ ___
   8   23   4   11   20   1
   ___ ___ ___ ___

4. A ___ ___ ___ ___ makes this sound.
   17   20   1   1
   ___ ___ ___ ___

5. ___ ___ ___ ___ ___ ___ o'clock
   9   12   20   1   11   20
   ___ ___ ___ ___

6. The opposite of ___ ___ ___
   17   16   19
   ___ ___ ___

### ≋BONUS≋
How many other words can you make from **IGUANODON**? Set a timer for two minutes. Then write down as many additional words as you can. When the time is up, compare your word list to the lists of other players. Whoever comes up with the most words wins!

ow do you tell
dinosaur that
ou think it's
well? Use the
ecoder wheel
o reveal these
aw-some dinosaur
ompliments.

# DINOSAUR COMPLIMENTS

For this puzzle, line up
P with 24
on the decoder wheel.

7 23 3'26 13   9   1 17 15 16 2   14 23 26   1 9 3 26   13 7 13 1.

17   12 17 22 23   5 16 9 2   17'12   12 23   5 17 2 16 23 3 2   7 23 3.

17'21   26 9 24 2 23 26 – 26 23 3 22 12   7 23 3 26   14 17 22 15 13 26.

7 23 3'26 13   24 2 13 26 – 26 17 14 14 17 11!

17'12   1 2 17 11 19   21 7   22 13 11 19   23 3 2   14 23 26   7 23 3!

## ≥ BONUS ≤

What's your favorite dinosaur? Write down
five words to describe this dinosaur. Using the
decoder wheel, place these words in code.
Have a friend try to decode the list and
guess which dinosaur you're talking about.

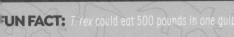

# DINO-MITE JOKES

The punch lines to these jokes are written in code. Using the decoder wheel, find the letter that matches the number under each blank space. Fill in the blanks until all the hidden punch lines are revealed.

For this puzzle, line up **A** with **22** on the decoder wheel.

**Who delivers Christmas presents to dinosaurs?**

___ ___ ___ ___ ___ ___ ___ ___ ___ ___
14  22  9  15  22  24  7  22  18  14

**What do dinosaurs wear when it's cold outside?**

___ ___ ___ ___ ___ ___ ___ ___ ___ ___ ___ ___ ___ ___
5  16  13  22  14  14  4  24  11  22  13  6  22  14

**What do you get when a dinosaur lays an egg on top of a mountain?**

___ ___ ___ ___ ___ ___ ___ ___ ___
22  9  26  2  2  13  10  7  7

**Where do dinosaurs go at night?**

___ ___ ___ ___ ___ ___ ___
15  10  14  7  26  26  11

**FUN FACT:** *T. rex* had holes in its skull that likely helped keep its brain cool.

These dinosaur riddles are real head-scratchers. And so are the answers to the riddles—that's because they're written in code! Read each riddle and try to guess its answer. Then use the decoder wheel to reveal if your guesses were right.

# RIP-ROARING RIDDLES

For this puzzle, line up
**Z** with **14**
on the decoder wheel.

## RIDDLE 1

I always look sharp,
it has to be said,
with the three horns and
frill on top of my head.

### WHO AM I?

\_\_ 6 23 17 19 6 15 8 3 4 7

## RIDDLE 2

I'm a large chunk of land,
a very ancient home.
On my hot, dry surface is
where dinosaurs first roamed.

### WHAT AM I?

4 15 2 21 19 15

## RIDDLE 3

While my dinosaur cousins
are stuck on the ground,
I can launch into the air and
soar all around.

### WHO AM I?

4 8 19 6 3 7 15 9 6

# HIDDEN PICTURES

For this puzzle, line up **D** with **25** on the decoder wheel.

There are eight objects hidden in the big picture. And each object name is hidden behind a code! Use the decoder wheel to uncover each object name. Once you've decoded them all, find the objects in the picture.

**TONGUE TWISTER:**
Ten thirteen-ton *Triceratops*.

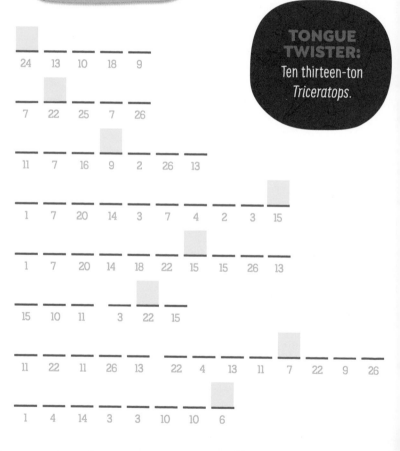

__ __ __ __ __
24 13 10 18 9

__ __ __ __ __
7 22 25 7 26

__ __ __ __ __ __ __
11 7 16 9 2 26 13

__ __ __ __ __ __ __ __ __ __
1 7 20 14 3 7 4 2 3 15

__ __ __ __ __ __ __ __ __
1 7 20 14 18 22 15 15 26 13

__ __ __ __ __ __
15 10 11 3 22 15

__ __ __ __ __ __ __ __ __ __ __ __ __
11 22 11 26 13 22 4 13 11 7 22 9 26

__ __ __ __ __ __ __
1 4 14 3 3 10 10 6

**FUN FACT:** Scientists think most dinosaur species have yet to be discovered!

# ⋝BONUS⋜

Read down the highlighted letters from the list
of objects to get the answer to the riddle below:

**What did the rock say to the dinosaur?**

**Nothing. Rocks** __ __ __ __ __ ' __ __ __ __ __ .

# ANSWERS

## PAGE 2

What did the green dinosaur say to the purple dinosaur?
**BREATHE**

What kind of music do paleontologists like?
**ROCK**

What do you ask a thirsty tyrannosaur?
**TEA, REX?**

What side of a dinosaur has the most scales?
**THE OUTSIDE**

## PAGE 3

Riddle 1
*STEGOSAURUS*

Riddle 2
**EGGS**

Riddle 3
**CARNIVORE**

## PAGES 4–5

CARROT
LOLLIPOP
PIZZA
WHEEL
FISH
BOOT
MUG
FLOWER

**BONUS:** Why is *Therizinosaurus* always showing off its long claws?
**Because they're CLAW-SOME!**

## PAGE 6

1. **RODENT, RAT**
2. **MEOWS, CAT**
3. **COLD, ICE**
4. **FRUIT, PEAR**
5. **HEAR, EARS**
6. **WEAR, CAPE**

## PAGE 7

| | |
|---|---|
| JAWS | BONES |
| REPTILE | DIG |
| EXTINCT | JURASSIC |

## PAGE 8

What did the dinosaur use to make hot dogs?
**JURASSIC PORK**

What dinosaur loves astrology?
**SKY-CERATOPS**

What did *Stegosaurus* say after making a mess in the kitchen?
**"DINO-SORRY!"**

What do you call a dinosaur who snores?
**A SNORE-A-SAURUS**

## PAGE 9

Dear Drake the *Diplodocus*,

I saw a **ROAR-SOME** concert today. First, a group of **RAPTORS** took the stage. Then a **DINO-CHORUS** sang. Finally, there was **JAWS** music. Everyone was super **TALON-TED**. Next time, you'll have **TOOTH** come along.

Yours ptero-ly,
Owen the *Oviraptor*

## PAGES 10–11

SAUCEPAN
MALLET
CROWN
BINOCULARS
COMB
CRESCENT MOON
RULER
SHOE

**BONUS:** Why do museums have old dinosaur bones?
**They can't afford NEW BONES!**

# ANSWERS

## PAGE 12

1. CHEW, GUM
2. LOWER, LEGS
3. STICKY, GLUE
4. TAG, GAME
5. WALL, MURAL
6. EAT, MEALS

## PAGE 13

YOU'RE T. REX-ELLENT!
I'M EN-RAPTOR-ED BY YOU.
I DIG YOU.
YOU MAKE MY HEART SAUR.
NOTHING *TRICERATOPS* YOU!

## PAGE 14

How do baby dinosaurs hatch?
**THEY EGGS-IT.**

What did the *T. rex* wish for when he blew out his candles?
**LONGER ARMS**

What did the fossil bring to dinner?
**SPARE RIBS**

What is a paleontologist's favorite book?
**THE DIG-TIONARY**

## PAGE 15

Riddle 1
**FOSSIL**

Riddle 2
**SPINOSAURUS**

Riddle 3
**TYRANNOSAURUS REX**

## PAGES 16–17

FEATHER
SCISSORS
HORSESHOE
PENNANT
GLOVE
RING
PARTY HAT

**BONUS:** Why was school easier for the dinosaurs?
**Because there was not much HISTORY to study.**

## PAGE 18

1. BEAR, CUB
2. YELLOW, BUS
3. CHARGE, BOSS
4. SIXTY, HOUR
5. BABY, CRIB
6. SNAKE, COBRA

## PAGE 19

| | |
|---|---|
| SCALES | HORN |
| CLAWS | TRIASSIC |
| FOSSIL | EGGS |

## PAGE 20

What do you call a dinosaur who hates losing?
**A SAUR LOSER**

What's a dinosaur's least favorite reindeer?
**COMET**

What do you call a dinosaur who knows a lot of words?
**A THESAURUS**

What do you call a dinosaur who just ran a marathon?
**DINO-SORE**

## PAGE 21

Dear Grandma,

Thank you for my **HATCH**-day gift! I was so **EGG-CITED** to get tickets to the Dinosaur Sports **CHOMP-IONSHIP**! I had so much fun, and my team **SAUR**-ed to victory. I **MISS** you and hope you **STOMP** by for a visit soon!

Love,
Eddie the *Edmontosaurus*

# ANSWERS

## PAGES 22–23

BAT
SAILBOAT
HEART
BOTTLE
MITTEN
CANDLE
LIGHT BULB
GLOVE

**BONUS:** Why did carnivorous dinosaurs eat their meat raw?
**Because they didn't know how to BARBECUE.**

## PAGE 24

1. **TWO, DUO**
2. **WOOFS, DOG**
3. **SHOVEL, DIG**
4. **BELL, DING**
5. **TWELVE, NOON**
6. **BAD, GOOD**

## PAGE 25

YOU'RE A SIGHT FOR SAUR EYES.
I DINO WHAT I'D DO WITHOUT YOU.
I'M RAPTOR-ROUND YOUR FINGER.
YOU'RE PTER-RIFFIC!
I'D STICK MY NECK OUT FOR YOU!

## PAGE 26

Who delivers Christmas presents to dinosaurs?
**SANTA CLAWS**

What do dinosaurs wear when it's cold outside?
**JURASSIC PARKAS**

What do you get when a dinosaur lays an egg on top of a mountain?
**AN EGG ROLL**

Where do dinosaurs go at night?
**TO SLEEP**

## PAGE 27

Riddle 1
*TRICERATOPS*

Riddle 2
**PANGEA**

Riddle 3
**PTEROSAUR**

## PAGES 28–29

CROWN
LADLE
PLUNGER
FLASHLIGHT
FLYSWATTER
TOP HAT
PAPER AIRPLANE
FISHHOOK

**BONUS:** What did the rock say to the dinosaur?
**Nothing. Rocks CAN'T TALK.**

For information about permission to reprint selections from this book, please contact permissions@highlights.com.

Published by Highlights Press
815 Church Street
Honesdale, Pennsylvania 18431
ISBN: 978-1-64472-845-1
Manufactured in Dongguan, Guangdong, China
Mfg. 08/2022
First edition
Visit our website at Highlights.com.
10 9 8 7 6 5 4 3 2 1